TURNING HEARTACHE INTO M.O.N.E.Y

<hr>

(MAKING OPPORTUNITIES NOW EVERYWHERE YEAR-ROUND)

<hr>

Tarrent 'Authur' Henry

Tarrent
AuthurHenry

Contents

Introduction

In the tapestry of our lives, heartache often stands as a formidable thread, weaving its presence into the fabric of our experiences. Yet, within the intricate patterns of adversity lies the potential for transformation—transforming heartache into a source of empowerment, prosperity, and purpose. Welcome to "Turning Heartache into M.O.N.E.Y.," a journey that transcends the boundaries of pain and illuminates the possibilities that emerge when we choose to reshape our narratives.

This book is not just a collection of pages but a compass guiding you through the profound exploration of personal and financial growth. It acknowledges the universal truth that heartache is an inevitable part of the human experience. However, it doesn't stop at mere acknowledgment; it propels you forward, offering insights, strategies, and real-life stories that inspire the transformative journey that awaits.

Unveiling the Power of Transformation

The opening chapter delves into the art of making—making something meaningful out of the fragments of heartache. We explore the birth of ideas, the crafting of a vision, and the importance of those initial steps toward transformation. **"Making"** is the inception, the spark that ignites the flame of possibility, signaling that within every heartache lies the potential for creation.

"**Opportunities**" beckons you to recognize the hidden gems concealed within adversity. The narrative unfolds as a guide to adopting an opportunistic mindset, seizing chances for growth, and maximizing your potential. As we journey through the exploration of possibilities, the understanding deepens that transformation is not just about weathering storms but harnessing the winds of change to set sail toward new horizons.

Embracing the Present

Chapter Three, aptly titled "**Now,**" invites you to inhabit the present moment. It explores the power of mindfulness, encouraging intentional living and the active utilization of current resources. This chapter serves as a reminder that the transformative journey is not a distant aspiration but a process unfolding in the present, urging you to take those decisive steps toward a brighter future, now.

The vast landscape of possibilities expands in Chapter Four, "**Everywhere.**" Opportunities are not confined to specific domains; they exist in entrepreneurship, creativity, global perspectives, and the intersection of passion and profit. "Everywhere" challenges preconceived limitations, prompting you to explore uncharted territories and recognize the myriad possibilities scattered across the landscape of your own potential.

A Year-Round Commitment to Transformation

As we reach the fifth chapter, "**Year-Round,**" the narrative transitions to the concept of a perpetual journey. Transformation is not a one-time event but a year-round commitment to personal and financial growth. The metaphor of seasons underscores the cyclical nature of personal development, emphasizing adaptability, resilience, and a legacy of purposeful living.

This book is an invitation to embark on a transformative odyssey—a journey where every setback becomes a stepping stone, every opportunity a chance for growth, and every moment an opportunity to shape a more prosperous and purposeful life. The narrative unfolds, not just within these pages, but in the choices, you make, the actions you take, and the mindset you cultivate beyond the confines of this book.

So, as you turn the pages, immerse yourself in the stories, reflect on the insights, and envision the possibilities that await. The journey from heartache to "**M.O.N.E.Y.**", is not just a narrative; it's an unfolding reality that you have the power to shape. Welcome to transformative exploration—a journey that invites you to turn the challenges of your past into the stepping stones of your future.

CHAPTER ONE

Making

"In the echoes of heartache, a resilient spirit awakens, ready to transform pain into purpose through the profound act of making."

In the quaint town of Everwood, nestled between rolling hills and whispering trees, lived a young woman named Elara. Her life, once adorned with the vibrant hues of love and companionship, now echoed with the melancholic notes of heartache. Elara's world shattered when her long-time partner decided to embark on a different path, leaving her to navigate the debris of a broken relationship.

As Elara wandered through the autumnal streets, the air thick with the scent of fallen leaves, she found solace in the most unexpected of places—an old bookstore known as "Elysium Pages." Its creaking wooden door opened to a world of dusty tomes and the comforting aroma of aged paper. Elara felt an unspoken connection with the books lining the shelves—a silent understanding that, like her, they held stories of resilience, transformation, and the ability to make something beautiful out of the fragments of the past.

One day, as Elara idly flipped through the pages of a weathered journal, a spark ignited within her. The pain that had once held her captive now became the catalyst for creation. She began pouring her emotions onto the pages, weaving a tapestry of words that depicted the highs and lows of her journey. The journal transformed into a vessel for her thoughts, dreams, and vision for a future yet to unfold.

As the ink danced on the paper, Elara's pain metamorphosed into the birth of ideas. The act of journaling became a cathartic process, and with each stroke of the pen, she began to see a glimmer of a new beginning. The pages, once blank, now held the blueprint for a venture that would encapsulate her newfound strength—a candle-making business infused with the scents of resilience, hope, and renewal.

The process of making candles became Elara's sanctuary. In the quiet corners of her kitchen, she blended fragrances that mirrored her emotional journey—lavender for healing, vanilla for comfort, and eucalyptus for rejuvenation. The flickering flames of the candles mirrored the sparks of creativity that had ignited within her.

Word of Elara's unique candles spread throughout Everwood, finding resonance with others who sought solace in the dance of candlelight. Elysium Pages, once just a haven for forgotten books, now hosted Elara's creations. The cozy bookstore became a sanctuary not just for stories but for the tangible embodiment of one woman's resilience and ability to make something beautiful out of heartache.

Elara's candle-making venture thrived, not just as a business but as a symbol of the transformative power within. With each sale, she reclaimed a piece of herself, turning her pain into purpose. The once-shattered artist had become a creator, and her candles whispered stories of renewal to those who chose to listen.

Elara's journey illustrates that making is not just about tangible creations; it's about transforming the intangible—pain, emotions, and experiences—into something that resonates with the world. The scent of her candles permeated Everwood, a fragrant reminder that out of the ashes of heartache, one can craft a story of strength, creativity, and the unwavering spirit of making.

Resurgence: Crafting Beauty from Heartache

In the bustling city of Lumina, where skyscrapers kissed the clouds and neon lights painted the streets, lived a young woman named Isabella. Her life had been a symphony of joy, with a promising career in the world of digital art and a loving partner by her side. However, the melody abruptly shifted when a heartbreaking breakup left Isabella in the silent aftermath of shattered dreams.

Amid the urban hustle, Isabella found herself drawn to an old art studio tucked away in a hidden alley—a place known as "Artisan's Haven." Its weathered sign swung gently in the breeze, inviting her to step into a world where creativity and healing intertwined. Inside, the air was thick with the scent of paint, and the flickering light of old-fashioned lamps created an atmosphere of serenity.

As Isabella explored the studio, she stumbled upon an assortment of discarded wooden pallets. An idea began to blossom within her—a vision to breathe life into these forgotten fragments and create something extraordinary. Isabella's pain, like the raw wood before her, was waiting to be transformed into a masterpiece.

With determination in her heart, Isabella started her journey of making. Armed with a chisel, a mallet, and her vivid imagination, she began to sculpt the wood into intricate shapes. Each strike of the chisel echoed her determination to reshape her narrative. The process became a therapeutic dance, a tangible expression of her emotions, and a way to make sense of the fragments of her heart.

As the weeks passed, Isabella's studio became a sanctuary of creation. The wooden pallets evolved into a stunning sculpture—a phoenix rising from the ashes, symbolic of her own rebirth. The sculpture stood tall, its wings outstretched, capturing the essence of resilience, transformation, and the indomitable spirit of making.

Word of Isabella's creation spread like wildfire in Lumina's artistic circles. Artisan's Haven transformed into a gallery showcasing her masterpiece. The sculpture, now named "Resurgence," became a symbol of hope for those who had faced heartache. People flocked to witness the embodiment of Isabella's journey—a journey of turning pain into art, heartache into healing.

The resonance of "Resurgence" extended beyond the art world. Isabella began receiving commissions to create bespoke sculptures for others navigating their own heartaches. Each piece told a unique story, a testament to the power of creation in the face of adversity. Isabella, once a victim of heartbreak, had become a creator, shaping her pain into something that resonated with others.

Isabella's story illustrates that making is a profound act of transformation. It's about taking the broken pieces of one's life and crafting them into something beautiful and meaningful. Isabella's sculptures became more than art—they became beacons of resilience, guiding others through their own journey of pain and creation. The art studio, once a refuge for the broken-hearted, had become a testament to the extraordinary power of making.

As you navigate through these pages, you are encouraged to embrace your own creative sparks. Whether it's a business idea, a passion project, or a newfound purpose, the journey from heartache to M.O.N.E.Y. begins with the spark of an idea, a glimmer of light amidst emotional darkness.

Crafting a Vision

The act of making is not haphazard; it requires intention and vision. In this chapter, we explore the importance of crafting a vision from the fragments of heartache. These stories unfold not as a series of random events but as a deliberate and purposeful construction. Through introspection and determination, a vision was shaped that transcended the pain, laying the foundation for a future that defied the constraints of heartbreak.

You are prompted to reflect on your own vision. What can you create from the broken pieces in your life? How can a new narrative be woven from the threads of your sorrow? This chapter encourages you to take a proactive approach to shaping your vision, a roadmap for your transformative journey that is up ahead.

Taking the First Steps

The power of making lies not just in the idea or the vision but in the courage to take the first steps. Your journey will be marked by those initial strides—timid yet resolute. The pain that once immobilized you will now propel you forward. Let this chapter serve as your guide, urging you to embrace the discomfort of the unknown and step into the realm of possibility.

The first steps are not always grand; they are often humble and tentative. Yet, they are the foundation upon which the entire edifice of transformation is built. Through these stories, you have witnessed the significance of action, of turning aspirations into reality one step at a time.

Transforming Pain into Purpose

Ultimately, the essence of making is the transformation of pain into purpose. In the crucible of heartache, a new purpose is forged—a purpose that goes beyond personal healing to contribute something meaningful to the world. Your journey will exemplify the alchemy of turning the lead of heartbreak into the gold of purposeful living.

As you conclude this first chapter, the message is clear: the power to make, to transform, and to innovate resides within. This chapter lays the groundwork for the odyssey ahead, where heartache becomes the raw material for a masterpiece yet to be revealed. The story unfolds, and with each turn of the page, you are invited to discover your own capacity for making something extraordinary out of the ordinary pain of the human experience.

CHAPTER HIGHLIGHTS

1. **The Birth of Ideas**

    - In the aftermath of heartache, the chapter explores how quiet moments become fertile grounds for the birth of ideas. Elara's cathartic act of scribbling in a notebook serves as a testament to the potential for innovation and creativity in the face of emotional darkness. You are encouraged to recognize your own creative spark and the transformative power of ideas.

2. **Crafting a Vision**

    - Making is portrayed as a deliberate and purposeful act that requires crafting a vision from the fragments of heartache. Elara's story unfolds as an intentional construction, laying the foundation for a future that transcends pain. The chapter prompts you to reflect on shaping your own vision and narrative, highlighting the importance of intention in the transformative journey.

3. **Taking the First Steps**

  - The power of making is not just in ideas or vision but in the courage to take the first steps. Elara's journey is marked by humble yet resolute initial strides, propelled forward by the pain that once immobilized her. You are guided to embrace the discomfort of the unknown and understand the significance of action in turning aspirations into reality.

4. **Transforming Pain into Purpose**

  - The essence of making is portrayed as the transformation of pain into purpose. In the crucible of heartache, a new purpose is forged—a purpose that goes beyond personal healing to contribute something meaningful to the world. Isabella's journey exemplifies the alchemy of turning heartbreak into purposeful living, inspiring you to consider your own capacity for transformation.

5. **Empowerment and Self-Discovery**

  - Chapter One serves as an empowering invitation for you to recognize the untapped potential within yourself. It celebrates the human spirit's ability to create, innovate, and build even in the face of profound sadness. The chapter encourages you to embark on a journey of self-discovery, where the act of making becomes a means of uncovering resilience and creative forces within.

THOUGHT QUESTIONS

1. What role does creativity play in the process of turning heartache into opportunity?

   - Reflect on the various creative outlets explored in the chapter, such as Emily's notebook scribblings. How does creativity serve as a catalyst for transforming pain into purpose?

2. In what ways can the initial steps taken during moments of heartache influence the trajectory of one's transformation journey?

   - Consider the significance of the first steps discussed in the chapter. How do these early actions set the tone for the rest of the transformation process, and what do they signify in terms of personal agency and resilience?

3. Explore the concept of making as an active response to heartache. How does the act of creating something new contribute to the healing process?

   - Examine the therapeutic aspect of making and how it helps you navigate through your emotional turmoil. In what ways can the act of creation become a form of self-expression and healing?

4. What role does vision play in the transformation from heartache to M.O.N.E.Y.?

   - Delve into the importance of crafting a vision, as highlighted in the chapter. How does having a clear vision contribute to a sense of purpose and direction, especially in the face of adversity?

5. Consider the idea that making is not just about tangible creations but also about taking the first steps toward transformation. How do these initial actions contribute to personal growth and resilience?

   - Explore the broader implications of making, beyond the physical or tangible outcomes. How do the first steps represent a commitment to change and personal development?

Opportunities

"In the shadows of adversity, opportunities await their unveiling, beckoning us to seize the unseen possibilities and turn them into pathways of growth and success."

In the wake of heartache, when the world seems cloaked in shadows, there exists a subtle but powerful light—the light of opportunities waiting to be uncovered. Chapter Two of "Turning Heartache into M.O.N.E.Y." invites you to explore this realm of possibilities, to recognize that adversity often conceals unexpected chances for growth and success.

Navigating the Uncharted Seas of Change

In the vibrant coastal town of Harbor Haven, where the sea breeze carried whispers of untold stories, lived a spirited woman named Olivia. Her life, once anchored in a secure corporate job, was abruptly set adrift when the company faced restructuring, and she found herself among the many casualties of downsizing.

Amid the initial waves of uncertainty, Olivia chose to view her situation not as a setback but as an uncharted sea of opportunities. She decided to return to her childhood passion for photography, a dream she had tucked away in the recesses of her heart while navigating the demands of her previous career.

With camera in hand, Olivia set out to capture the essence of Harbor Haven—the sunsets painting the sky in hues of coral and lavender, the fishermen weaving their tales on the docks, and the laughter of children echoing through the quaint streets. What started as a therapeutic escape soon unfolded into an unexpected opportunity.

One day, while perusing the local café, Olivia's keen eye caught the attention of a gallery owner. The owner, intrigued by the raw emotion captured in Olivia's photographs, offered her a chance to showcase her work. The gallery became Olivia's canvas, and her photographs, the brushstrokes that painted the narrative of her newfound journey.

As word spread about Olivia's exhibition, doors previously unseen began to creak open. Local businesses sought her artistic touch for promotional campaigns, and soon, Olivia found herself not only rediscovering her passion but also turning it into a viable business. The very downsizing that once seemed like a stormy sea had, in fact, ushered her into a harbor of unexpected opportunities.

Emboldened by her success, Olivia took another leap—she launched photography workshops for the youth in Harbor Haven. Through her lens, she taught them to see the world with a fresh perspective, nurturing a new generation of artists. The workshops not only became a source of joy for Olivia but also a testament to the transformative power of seizing opportunities.

The ripple effect of Olivia's choices reached beyond the shores of Harbor Haven. Her story resonated with those facing similar crossroads, inspiring them to recognize the latent opportunities in their own challenges. Olivia, once confined by the four walls of a corporate office, had discovered a vast horizon of possibilities by simply opening herself to the opportunities disguised within adversity.

Olivia's journey illuminates the profound truth that opportunities often emerge from the unlikeliest of circumstances. It's a narrative that encourages readers to embrace change not as a threat but as a kaleidoscope of undiscovered possibilities. Olivia's story becomes a beacon, guiding others to navigate the sea of opportunities that dances beyond the horizon when one is willing to set sail into the unknown.

Embracing Opportunities in the Tapestry of Change

In the bustling city of Skylight Springs, where towering skyscrapers kissed the clouds, lived a determined young man named Ethan. His days were once defined by the rhythm of a monotonous job in a crowded office until an unexpected turn of events shattered the routine he had known. The company he worked for went bankrupt, leaving him at the crossroads of uncertainty.

Rather than succumbing to despair, Ethan saw this upheaval as an opportunity for reinvention. He had always possessed a flair for storytelling, often weaving narratives in the quiet corners of his apartment. With a newfound sense of purpose, he decided to dive headfirst into the world of freelance writing.

As Ethan navigated the labyrinth of online platforms, he stumbled upon a unique opportunity—a call for submissions from a renowned digital magazine seeking fresh perspectives on urban living. Drawing inspiration from the challenges he faced during the company's closure, Ethan penned a heartfelt piece that resonated with the essence of resilience and adaptability.

To his surprise, his article was not only accepted but garnered attention from a literary agent who saw potential in his storytelling prowess. This serendipitous encounter opened the door to a world of possibilities Ethan had never imagined. The literary agent offered to represent him, presenting the chance to turn his passion for writing into a full-fledged career.

Embracing the momentum, Ethan delved into writing a novel that mirrored his own journey—a tale of an individual navigating the tumultuous waves of change and discovering unexpected opportunities amidst the chaos. The novel gained traction, attracting the interest of a publishing house eager to bring his story to a broader audience.

As Ethan's literary endeavors flourished, he seized another opportunity that unfolded before him. Recognizing the hunger for authentic narratives, he founded a platform to amplify the voices of those facing life-altering transitions. Skylight Chronicles, as he named it, became a digital haven where stories of resilience, transformation, and seizing opportunities found a home.

The platform quickly gained popularity, attracting contributors from around the globe. Ethan's journey, from the confines of a corporate office to the helm of a storytelling revolution, became an inspiring narrative for those navigating their paths in a rapidly changing world.

Ethan's story illuminates the transformative power embedded in unexpected opportunities. It serves as a reminder that even in the face of adversity, there exists a tapestry of chances waiting to be woven into the fabric of one's success. Ethan's journey becomes a beacon, encouraging readers to embrace change as a canvas for new beginnings and untapped opportunities.

The Art of Identifying Opportunity

Identifying opportunities requires a keen eye and an open mind. Delving into the art of recognizing potential where others see only obstacles.

Opportunities may not always come gift-wrapped; sometimes, they are disguised as challenges. Through reflection and introspection, you will uncover opportunities concealed within your own struggles, empowering you to turn adversity into a launching pad for future success.

Maximizing Opportunities

Seizing opportunities is only the first step; maximizing your potential is where true transformation occurs. You are prompted to assess your own strengths and resources, understanding that the successful exploitation of opportunities often requires a combination of skill, timing, and perseverance. By exploring various avenues, from career changes to personal development, you are encouraged to embark on your own journey of opportunity maximization.

Cultivating an Opportunistic Mindset

Beyond specific strategies, cultivating an opportunistic mindset must become a recurring theme. You will be challenged to adopt a perspective that actively seeks out possibilities in every situation. Drawing parallels between personal anecdotes and broader principles, you are encouraged to develop a mental framework that turns setbacks into stepping stones and failures into lessons.

The stories within this chapter underscore that cultivating an opportunistic mindset is not a passive endeavor but an active choice. It requires a commitment to continuous learning, adaptability, and the courage to embrace change. As you absorb these lessons, you will begin to see the landscape of opportunities as an ever-expanding canvas awaiting your creative strokes.

Opportunities as Catalysts for Transformation

Ultimately, when seized and maximized, opportunities become powerful catalysts for transformation. Through your unseen lens, you witness the metamorphosis of pain being transformed into prosperity.

The overarching message is clear: in the realm of turning heartache into M.O.N.E.Y., opportunities are not just chances for financial gain but vehicles for personal growth and fulfillment.

As we conclude Chapter Two, carry with you the understanding that the journey from heartache to M.O.N.E.Y. is not a linear path but a dynamic process of continuous discovery. Opportunities abound, waiting to be recognized, seized, and transformed into the building blocks of a brighter future.

CHAPTER HIGHLIGHTS

1. **Seizing the Unseen**

   - The chapter introduces the idea that opportunities often lie hidden within the challenges of heartache. Real-life vignettes, including Olivia's story, illustrate how you can discover unforeseen possibilities in the wake of adversity. You are prompted to reassess your own struggles, viewing them as potential bridges to unexplored opportunities.

2. **The Art of Identifying Opportunity**

   - The narrative delves into the art of recognizing opportunities amid adversity. Through real-life examples, you learn to discern the silver lining in challenges and cultivate your own opportunities. This chapter encourages a mindset shift, guiding you to see adversity not as a dead end but as a diverging path leading to unexplored possibilities.

3. **Maximizing Opportunities**

   - Seizing opportunities is just the beginning; maximizing your potential is where transformation occurs. The chapter serves as a practical guide, offering strategies and insights on how to extract maximum value from opportunities. Olivia's journey becomes a blueprint, highlighting the importance of resilience, adaptability, and a forward-thinking mindset.

4. **Cultivating an Opportunistic Mindset**

    - Beyond specific strategies, the chapter emphasizes the cultivation of an opportunistic mindset. You are challenged to actively seek out possibilities in every situation, turning setbacks into stepping stones and failures into lessons. Personal anecdotes and broader principles underscore the active choice required to develop a mindset that embraces change and continuous learning.

5. **Opportunities as Catalysts for Transformation**

    - The overarching message of the chapter is that opportunities, when seized and maximized, become powerful catalysts for transformation. Through various narratives, readers witness how pain can be transformed into prosperity. Opportunities are portrayed not just as chances for financial gain but as vehicles for personal growth and fulfillment.

THOUGHT QUESTIONS

1. How does the chapter challenge traditional notions of adversity by presenting it as a gateway to opportunities?

   - Reflect on the stories shared in the chapter that highlight individuals who found opportunities within adversity. In what ways does this perspective shift the narrative around challenges and setbacks?

2. Explore the concept of opportunity identification. How can you cultivate a mindset that allows you to recognize potential within challenges?

   - Consider the anecdotes in the chapter where you identified opportunities in unexpected places. What skills or attitudes contribute to the ability to see opportunities where others might see obstacles?

3. In what ways does the chapter emphasize the importance of maximizing opportunities once they are identified?

   - Delve into the strategies and insights provided in the chapter for maximizing opportunities. How do these stories illustrate the transformative power of seizing and maximizing the potential within opportunities?

4. Examine the connection between seizing opportunities and personal growth. How can you leverage opportunities as catalysts for a broader transformation in your life?

   - Reflect on the personal development journeys depicted in the chapter. How do these journeys demonstrate that seizing opportunities goes beyond immediate gains and contributes to overall growth and fulfillment?

5. Consider the idea of an opportunistic mindset. How can you actively cultivate a mindset that actively seeks out possibilities in every situation?

   - Explore the narratives that highlight the cultivation of an opportunistic mindset. What specific behaviors or habits can you adopt to foster a mindset that turns setbacks into stepping stones and failures into lessons?

Now

"In the present moment lies the canvas of transformation, urging us to embrace 'Now' as the foundation for turning heartache into a tapestry of resilience, growth, and empowered living."

In the aftermath of heartache, the present moment emerges as a potent force—a canvas upon which the future is painted. Chapter Three of "Turning Heartache into M.O.N.E.Y." shifts the focus to the immediacy of "Now," urging readers to embrace the present as the foundation for transformation. This chapter serves as a compass, guiding individuals through the intricacies of living in the now while navigating the journey from pain to prosperity.

Embracing Harmony in the Present

In the tranquil town of Serenity Grove, where time seemed to slow to the rhythm of nature, lived a woman named Clara. Her life had been a series of meticulously planned steps, a dance to the tune of routine and predictability. However, a health scare shook the foundation of her structured existence, casting her into the uncertain terrain of the present moment.

As Clara sat in the quiet garden of her cottage, the fragrant blooms and rustling leaves whispered a compelling truth—the only certainty in life is the now. Inspired by this realization, Clara embarked on a journey of mindfulness and intentional living. Instead of dwelling on the uncertainties of the future, she committed herself to savoring the beauty of each passing moment.

Guided by the gentle cadence of nature, Clara immersed herself in simple pleasures—the warmth of sunlight on her skin, the melody of birdsong, and the soothing rhythm of her own breath. She discovered a newfound appreciation for the small details that often eluded a hurried gaze. In the now, Clara found solace, a sanctuary from the anxieties that once clouded her days.

Embracing the philosophy of now, Clara also sought to mend strained relationships and nurture connections that had faded into the background. She reached out to old friends, mended bridges with family, and cultivated a sense of community in Serenity Grove. Each interaction became a celebration of shared moments, an acknowledgment of the precious now that bound them together.

But Clara's journey extended beyond personal introspection. She became an advocate for mindfulness in Serenity Grove, organizing workshops and events to share the transformative power of living in the now. The community embraced these sessions, creating a ripple effect that touched the lives of individuals seeking a reprieve from the pressures of an uncertain future.

In the midst of her newfound purpose, Clara also recognized the financial implications of living in the now. She reevaluated her career choices, focusing on endeavors that aligned with her passions and values. This shift not only brought her a sense of fulfillment but also opened unexpected avenues for financial stability.

As Clara embraced the now, her health improved, relationships flourished, and a sense of peace permeated every aspect of her life. The journey from a life dictated by routine to a life shaped by the now became a testament to the transformative power of mindfulness.

Clara's journey is an invitation to step into the now, where the beauty of life unfolds in every breath, every heartbeat, and every shared moment.

Cultivating Prosperity in the Present Moment

In the bustling metropolis of Urbania, where the city's heartbeat echoed in the rhythm of hurried footsteps, lived a man named Leo. His life, once a whirlwind of deadlines and perpetual motion, came to an abrupt standstill when he faced a sudden job loss. Amid the disorienting stillness that followed, Leo found an unexpected gift— the opportunity to live in the now.

With a severance package in hand and a heart open to new possibilities, Leo decided to embark on a journey of self-discovery. He enrolled in meditation classes, seeking solace in the ancient practice of mindfulness. As the minutes turned into hours of guided breath and focused presence, Leo learned to silence the cacophony of worries about the future.

In the heart of Urbania's concrete jungle, Leo discovered a hidden gem—a community garden nestled between towering skyscrapers. The garden became his sanctuary, a green oasis where time seemed to slow down. Surrounded by the vibrant colors of blooming flowers and the soothing sounds of nature, Leo embraced the now with a newfound appreciation for life's simple pleasures.

Leo's journey took an unexpected turn when he encountered a group of like-minded individuals in the garden—people who, like him, were navigating the uncertainties of the present. They formed a close-knit community, sharing stories, supporting one another, and finding joy in the shared experience of living in the now.

Inspired by the transformative power of mindfulness and community, Leo initiated a series of "Now Workshops" in Urbania. These workshops became a refuge for those grappling with the anxieties of an unpredictable future. Participants learned to ground themselves in the present, fostering a sense of calm and resilience that transcended the challenges they faced.

Leo's commitment to living in the now extended beyond personal well-being. He explored entrepreneurial ventures that aligned with his newfound values, launching a sustainable urban gardening initiative. The project not only brought beauty to the cityscape but also provided a source of income for Leo and other members of the community.

As word spread about Leo's journey and the Now Workshops, a movement began to take shape in Urbania. The city, once defined by its relentless pace, started to embrace a collective shift toward mindfulness and intentional living. The now became a precious commodity, a shared currency that enriched the lives of individuals and the community at large.

Leo's journey becomes a guide, showing that in the now, even amidst uncertainty, one can find clarity, connection, and the seeds of a prosperous future.

The Power of Presence

"Now" is not merely a moment on the timeline but a powerful dimension where decisions are made, actions are taken, and transformations unfold. The narrative unfolds as readers are introduced to the concept of mindfulness—the art of being fully present in the current moment. Through the lens of real-life experiences and contemplative reflection, this chapter explores how a conscious presence can become a catalyst for change.

As you immerse yourself in the stories within this chapter, you are encouraged to appreciate the significance of the present moment. It becomes a canvas on which you can paint the first strokes of your transformation, acknowledging that the choices made now have the potential to shape a brighter future.

Navigating the Landscape of Now

The journey from heartache to M.O.N.E.Y. requires a deliberate navigation of the "Now." This chapter unfolds as a guide, offering practical insights and strategies on how to leverage the current moment for personal and financial growth. Whether through skill development, networking, or embracing new opportunities, you are encouraged to explore the vast landscape of possibilities within the present.

The narrative emphasizes that the "Now" is not a passive state but an active arena where you can plant the seeds of your aspirations. Realizing that every action taken in the present is a step toward a more resilient and empowered future becomes a central theme, inspiring you to engage with the "Now" intentionally.

The Paradox of Patience and Urgency

In the quest for transformation, a delicate balance between patience and urgency must be struck. This chapter explores the paradox inherent in the "Now," emphasizing the importance of patience in allowing seeds to sprout while acknowledging the urgency to take decisive actions.

This chapter navigates the nuanced dance between patience and urgency, urging you to embrace the journey without succumbing to the impatience that often accompanies the desire for quick results. This delicate balance becomes a key theme, resonating with the understanding that sustainable transformation requires both time and timely action

Utilizing Resources in the Now

The "Now" is a treasure trove of resources waiting to be harnessed. From personal skills to external opportunities, this chapter delves into the idea that you can leverage existing resources to propel yourself forward.

You are prompted to conduct a resource inventory of your own, identifying the skills, connections, and opportunities available in the "Now." This chapter serves as a call to action, encouraging you to recognize that the power to transform lies not in some distant future but in the resources at your disposal in the present.

The Resilience of Now

As you navigate the journey of turning heartache into M.O.N.E.Y., the "Now" becomes a testing ground for resilience. Whether facing rejection, pivoting career paths, or navigating personal growth, you will learn that resilience is not a product of the past or a promise for the future but a quality honed in the crucible of the "Now."

Embrace these challenges as opportunities for growth, understanding that setbacks are not roadblocks but stepping stones in the transformative journey. As you internalize the resilience of the "Now," you are being equipped to face the uncertainties of the path ahead with a fortified spirit.

Living the Transformation Now

As you close this chapter, carry with you the understanding that the power to transform exists not in the past or future but in the choices made, actions taken, and mindset cultivated in the "Now." The narrative continues to unfold, and the journey from heartache to M.O.N.E.Y. gains momentum, propelled by the momentum of intentional living in the present.

CHAPTER HIGHLIGHTS

1. **The Power of Presence**

   - The chapter introduces the concept of mindfulness, highlighting the importance of being fully present in the current moment. It emphasizes that the "Now" is not just a moment in time but a powerful dimension where decisions and transformations unfold.

2. **Navigating the Landscape of Now**

   - Chapter Three serves as a practical guide for you, offering insights and strategies on how to leverage the present moment for personal and financial growth. It encourages deliberate actions, such as skill development, networking, and embracing new opportunities, within the current landscape.

3. **The Paradox of Patience and Urgency**

   - The chapter explores the delicate balance between patience and urgency in the journey of transformation. It underscores the paradox of patiently nurturing endeavors while acknowledging the urgency to take decisive actions. Real-life anecdotes illustrate the nuanced dance between these two elements.

4. **Utilizing Resources in the Now**

   - The "Now" is presented as a treasure trove of resources waiting to be harnessed. Through the example of Leo's journey, you are prompted to conduct your own resource inventory, identifying skills, connections, and opportunities available in the present.

5. **The Resilience of Now**

   - Resilience is portrayed as a quality cultivated in the present moment. The chapter unfolds with stories of setbacks and triumphs, illustrating how resilience is not a product of the past or a promise for the future but a quality honed in the crucible of the "Now."

THOUGHT QUESTIONS

1. How does the chapter emphasize the power of living in the present moment as a foundation for transformation?

   - Reflect on the concept of "Now" and its significance in the chapter. In what ways does being present in the moment serve as a canvas for shaping one's future?

2. Explore the balance between patience and urgency discussed in the chapter. How can you navigate this delicate equilibrium in their pursuit of transformation?

   - Consider the anecdotes that highlight the paradox of patience and urgency. How can you strike a balance between patiently nurturing your endeavors and taking decisive actions to drive change?

3. Examine the role of resilience in the "Now" as a testing ground for personal growth. How can setbacks and challenges in the present moment become opportunities for building resilience?

   - Reflect on the stories of resilience presented in the chapter. In what ways do challenges in the "Now" contribute to personal development and fortitude?

4. Consider the theme of utilizing resources in the present. How can you leverage your existing skills, connections, and opportunities to propel yourself forward?

   - Explore the examples of resource utilization provided in the chapter. How can you conduct a resource inventory in your own life and maximize the potential within your current circumstances?

5. Reflect on the concept of adaptability in the "Now" landscape. How does the chapter highlight the importance of being adaptable and open to change in the pursuit of transformation?

   - Delve into the stories that underscore the significance of adaptability. How can you embrace change and navigate the evolving landscape of the "Now" in your personal and professional life?

Everywhere

"In the vast landscape of possibilities, 'Everywhere' becomes the canvas of transformation, inviting us to explore diverse avenues and discover opportunities hidden in the uncharted territories of our potential."

In the expansive landscape of turning heartache into M.O.N.E.Y., Chapter Four unfolds as a panoramic view of opportunities, suggesting that transformation is not confined to specific realms but is omnipresent—everywhere. This chapter is an exploration of the diverse avenues available, beckoning you to consider the multitude of possibilities awaiting discovery in the uncharted territories of your own potential.

Painting Prosperity in Every Corner"

In the eclectic city of Harmony Junction, where diversity was celebrated on every street corner, lived a spirited artist named Maya. Her life had always been a canvas of creativity, but a sudden setback in the form of an art exhibition rejection left her questioning the expansiveness of her artistic journey. Little did Maya know that this rejection would become the catalyst for a transformative adventure that would redefine her understanding of opportunities.

Undeterred by the rejection, Maya decided to embark on a quest to discover inspiration everywhere. Armed with a sketchbook, she roamed the vibrant streets of Harmony Junction, finding artistic potential in the most unexpected places. From the murals adorning alleyways to the rhythmic patterns of everyday life, Maya embraced the philosophy that creativity could be found everywhere, waiting to be unveiled.

As Maya immersed herself in this newfound perspective, she stumbled upon a community art project that would change the trajectory of her artistic career. The project involved collaborating with local businesses to turn mundane spaces into artistic expressions. Maya's sketches, once confined to the pages of her sketchbook, now adorned walls, storefronts, and even utility boxes, transforming the city into an ever-evolving gallery.

The ripple effect of Maya's initiative extended beyond the canvas. Local businesses experienced increased foot traffic, and the community found a shared sense of pride in the vibrant transformation of their surroundings. Maya's artistic endeavor became a testament to the idea that opportunities were not limited to conventional spaces but could be found everywhere, waiting to be uncovered with a creative eye.

Inspired by the success of the community project, Maya took her artistic exploration to new heights—literally. She collaborated with architects to design visually stunning murals on rooftops, turning the city skyline into a breathtaking panorama of color and expression. The once-rejected artist had not only found opportunities in the rejection but had also woven her creativity into the very fabric of Harmony Junction.

Maya's journey of discovering opportunities everywhere wasn't confined to the artistic realm. She recognized the potential for collaboration in unexpected places—forging partnerships with local businesses, community organizations, and even city officials. Maya's story became an illustration of how a shift in perspective could turn setbacks into stepping stones and transform a once-rejected artist into a catalyst for positive change.

Maya's story serves as a vibrant canvas, depicting the boundless opportunities that exist everywhere. It encourages readers to look beyond the conventional, to see potential in the ordinary, and to recognize that the seeds of prosperity can be scattered across the landscape of life, waiting to be cultivated with a creative and open heart.

Blossoming Horizons

In the lively town of Radiant Springs, where the hustle and bustle of daily life harmonized with the rustle of leaves in the nearby woods, lived a woman named Livia. Her passion for gardening had transformed her backyard into a haven of blooms, and she had long dreamt of sharing this natural beauty with the community. However, a series of setbacks, including a failed business venture and personal challenges, had dimmed Livia's enthusiasm.

One day, as she wandered through the town's market square, Livia noticed a neglected corner that seemed to yearn for a touch of life. Instead of seeing an abandoned space, Livia envisioned a vibrant community garden—a place where neighbors could gather, children could play, and the aroma of blooming flowers could infuse joy into the air.

Determined to turn her vision into reality, Livia reached out to local businesses, seeking collaboration for her community garden project. To her surprise, the response was overwhelmingly positive. The corner that had once been overlooked became a canvas for creativity. Local artists contributed sculptures, businesses sponsored benches, and community members volunteered their time to bring Livia's dream to fruition.

As the community garden blossomed, Livia's vision expanded beyond the confines of Radiant Springs. She began hosting gardening workshops, sharing her knowledge with neighboring towns, and encouraging communities far and wide to transform neglected spaces into thriving gardens. Livia's story became a testament to the idea that opportunities for growth and prosperity were not limited to a single location—they were everywhere, waiting to be uncovered.

Inspired by the success of the community garden, Livia explored new opportunities in unexpected places. She collaborated with local schools to integrate gardening into the curriculum, fostering a sense of environmental stewardship among the younger generation. The community garden also became a venue for events, attracting visitors from neighboring towns and creating a ripple effect of economic growth.

As Livia's journey unfolded, the once-neglected corner in Radiant Springs became a symbol of resilience, creativity, and the potential for growth in every corner of life.

Livia's ability to see opportunities everywhere not only revitalized her passion but also transformed the community and beyond.

Livia's story invites readers to recognize that opportunities are not confined to specific locations or circumstances. Instead, they exist in the overlooked corners, waiting for individuals with a vision and determination to bring them to life. Livia's journey illustrates that by looking at the world with fresh eyes, one can uncover opportunities that are truly everywhere.

The Ubiquity of Opportunities

Opportunities are not constrained by boundaries; they exist everywhere. From entrepreneurial ventures to creative pursuits, the narrative expands to illustrate that the journey from heartache to M.O.N.E.Y. is not limited by industry, geography, or circumstance. You are encouraged to broaden your perspective, recognizing that opportunities are scattered like hidden gems in the vast expanse of their lives.

As we navigate through these stories, the recurring theme is that transformation can manifest in various forms, from launching a startup to pursuing artistic passions. The "Everywhere" concept challenges readers to question preconceived notions and consider unconventional paths that may lead to both personal and financial fulfillment.

Entrepreneurial Exploration

Within the "Everywhere" landscape, entrepreneurship emerges as a dynamic force for transformation. This chapter delves into the entrepreneurial spirit—a mindset that transcends traditional business endeavors. Whether starting a company, freelancing, or engaging in the gig economy, you are prompted to explore the entrepreneurial possibilities within your skill sets and passions.

Real-life examples provide insights into how you can turn your talents into lucrative ventures. The narrative encourages you to view yourself as an entrepreneur of your own life, capable of identifying and capitalizing on opportunities that align with your skills and aspirations.

Creativity Unleashed

Creativity is not confined to the realms of artistry; it permeates every facet of life. The idea is that creativity when harnessed, can be a powerful catalyst for transformation. You will be inspired to unlock your own creative potential.

"Everywhere" is a canvas where creative endeavors, whether in business, technology, or the arts, can flourish. You are prompted to recognize the creative energy within yourself and explore how it can be channeled into ventures that transcend the boundaries of convention.

Global Perspectives and Networks

"Everywhere" extends beyond individual pursuits and ventures into the global landscape. You are being encouraged to consider the interconnectedness of the world and explore avenues beyond your immediate surroundings.

The Intersection of Passion and Profit

Within the vast landscape of opportunities, the intersection of passion and profit becomes a focal point. This chapter is a guide for you to align your pursuits with your passions, recognizing that the most fulfilling opportunities often arise when personal interests converge with financial viability.

The Tapestry of Transformation Unfolding Everywhere

As Chapter Four comes to a close, may you carry with you the realization that the journey of turning heartache into M.O.N.E.Y. is a tapestry woven from the threads of opportunities scattered everywhere.

CHAPTER HIGHLIGHTS

1. **Diverse Opportunity Landscape**

    - The chapter emphasizes the diversity of opportunities, breaking free from constraints like industry, geography, or circumstance. Stories showcase success in unexpected places and fields, encouraging readers to broaden their perspectives.

2. Entrepreneurial Spirit Unleashed

- Entrepreneurship emerges as a dynamic force for transformation. The narrative delves into various entrepreneurial endeavors, urging you to explore your own entrepreneurial potential, whether through startups, freelancing, or engaging in the gig economy.

3. Creativity as a Catalyst

- Creativity is portrayed as a universal force that permeates all aspects of life, not just the arts. The chapter explores how creativity, when harnessed, can lead to innovative solutions in business, technology, and other fields.

4. Global Perspectives and Networks

- The narrative extends beyond individual pursuits, highlighting the importance of a global perspective. Stories of individuals leveraging international networks illustrate that opportunities are not confined by borders, encouraging readers to explore avenues beyond their immediate surroundings.

5. Passion and Profit Alignment

- The intersection of passion and profit becomes a central theme. Real-life examples demonstrate how individuals turned their personal interests into profitable ventures, inspiring you to reflect on your passions and consider how you can align them with financial success.

THOUGHT QUESTIONS

1. Reflect on the concept of opportunities being everywhere. How does this perspective challenge conventional ideas about where opportunities can be found?

   - Explore the stories in the chapter that highlight opportunities in unexpected places. How can you broaden your perspectives to recognize opportunities scattered throughout various aspects of life?

2. Examine the role of entrepreneurship in the "Everywhere" landscape. How does the chapter portray entrepreneurship as a dynamic force for transformation beyond traditional business endeavors?

   - Consider the entrepreneurial spirit discussed in the chapter. How can you embrace an entrepreneurial mindset in diverse areas of your life, beyond traditional business ventures?

3. Delve into the theme of creativity unleashed everywhere. How can you harness your creative potential in different facets of life, not just in artistic pursuits?

- Reflect on the stories that showcase creativity in various domains. In what ways can you unlock your creative energy to drive innovation in business, technology, or personal development?

4. Explore the global perspectives and networks highlighted in the chapter. How can a global mindset and diverse networks contribute to uncovering opportunities in unexpected places?

   - Consider the narratives that emphasize the interconnectedness of the world. How can you build a diverse network and seek inspiration from a variety of sources to discover opportunities on a global scale?

5. Reflect on the intersection of passion and profit in the "Everywhere" landscape. How can you align your pursuits with your passions to create meaningful and profitable opportunities?

   - Delve into the stories that depict individuals turning their passions into profitable ventures. How can you identify and capitalize on opportunities that align with your personal interests and values?

Year Round

"As the seasons change, 'Year Round' prosperity unfolds, reminding us that the journey from heartache to M.O.N.E.Y. is not a moment but a continuous dance of resilience, innovation, and sustained growth."

Chapter Five, aptly titled "Year Round," invites you to envision a life where the transformative journey is not confined to specific seasons but is a continuous, year-round commitment to growth and prosperity. This chapter serves as a compass, guiding you through the final steps of the journey, emphasizing sustainability, resilience, and the perpetual pursuit of a purposeful and prosperous existence.

Nurturing Prosperity Through Life's Seasons

In the picturesque village of Evergreen Valley, where each season painted the landscape in its own hues, lived a woman named Sophia. Her story was a tale of resilience and perpetual growth, much like the evergreen trees that adorned the valley. Having weathered the storms of personal challenges and financial setbacks, Sophia became a living testament to the transformative power of embracing life's seasons year-round.

Sophia's journey began in the heart of winter, a time when the village lay beneath a blanket of snow. Faced with unexpected financial hardships, she decided to tap into her passion for crafting handmade candles. The warmth and glow of her creations not only brought comfort to others during the cold months but also ignited a spark of entrepreneurship within Sophia.

As the snow melted and spring blossomed, so did Sophia's ambitions. She expanded her candle-making venture, infusing her products with scents that captured the essence of each season. Spring brought the fragrances of blooming flowers, summer carried the aroma of fresh citrus, autumn resonated with the warmth of spices, and winter enveloped everything in a comforting blend of vanilla and cedar. Sophia's candles became a reflection of the cyclical nature of life—each season a reminder of both challenges and opportunities.

Sophia's commitment to growth was not limited to her business. Recognizing the importance of financial literacy, she started hosting workshops in Evergreen Valley, teaching community members how to navigate the ebb and flow of their personal finances. Her workshops became a year-round resource, offering guidance on budgeting, investing, and planning for the future.

As the village embraced Sophia's teachings, her influence extended beyond Evergreen Valley. She collaborated with neighboring communities, creating a network of financial education that transcended geographical boundaries. Sophia's mission to empower individuals to navigate life's financial seasons year-round resonated with people from all walks of life.

Summer brought prosperity to Sophia's candle-making business. The demand for her handcrafted creations soared, allowing her to invest in eco-friendly practices and support local artisans. As the leaves changed colors in autumn, Sophia diversified her offerings, introducing seasonal gift sets and collaborating with local businesses to create unique, themed collections.

Sophia's journey reached its pinnacle as winter returned to Evergreen Valley. The year-round cycle of growth and adaptation had transformed her from a candle maker facing financial challenges into a community leader and financial educator. Her story became a beacon of inspiration, illustrating that the journey from heartache to prosperity was not a linear path but a perpetual, evolving adventure.

Sophia's story unfolds as a celebration of life's seasons. It is a narrative that encourages you to embrace the ebb and flow of challenges and opportunities, recognizing that the journey toward financial and personal prosperity is a year-round commitment. Sophia's candles, once symbols of comfort, had become emblems of resilience, growth, and the enduring spirit of turning every season into a source of strength and abundance.

A Year-Round Journey from Setbacks to Success

In the bustling city of Mentropolis, where the rhythm of life never ceased, lived a woman named Taya. Her journey was a testament to the resilience of the human spirit and the boundless opportunities that could be uncovered year-round.

Taya had faced setbacks and heartbreaks in her early career as a graphic designer. The competitive nature of the industry and a series of personal challenges left her questioning her path. However, Taya refused to be defined by her struggles. She decided to take a leap of faith and launch her own design consultancy.

As spring breathed life into the city, Taya's consultancy began to bloom. She sought inspiration from the vibrant colors and fresh energy of the season to infuse creativity into her projects. The workshop she conducted in collaboration with local artists became an annual event, bringing together budding designers and seasoned creatives to exchange ideas and foster a sense of community.

With the arrival of summer, Taya's consultancy reached new heights. The longer days and warm weather seemed to invigorate the city's entrepreneurial spirit. Taya took advantage of the season's buzz to organize design festivals, attracting clients and collaborators from diverse industries. Her ability to turn challenges into opportunities became a source of inspiration for emerging designers facing their own hurdles.

As autumn painted the city in hues of gold and crimson, Taya expanded her consultancy's reach. She embraced the changing landscape by diversifying her services and offering design solutions for businesses adapting to evolving markets. Taya's story became synonymous with adaptability, a reminder that, like the changing seasons, businesses could thrive through transformation.

Winter, with its festive charm, brought a sense of reflection to Taya. The year-round journey had not been without its challenges, but every obstacle had become a stepping stone to growth. As snowflakes adorned the city streets, Taya took the time to mentor aspiring designers, sharing her experiences and guiding them through the intricacies of the industry.

Taya's consultancy had become a beacon of creativity, resilience, and year-round prosperity. The cyclical nature of her success mirrored the changing seasons of Metropolis, where challenges were met with innovation, setbacks with adaptability, and every day held the potential for growth.

Taya's story radiates as a reflection of the enduring spirit of entrepreneurship. It is a celebration of the year-round commitment to turning dreams into reality, setbacks into opportunities, and the recognition that prosperity is not confined to a particular moment but is a continuous journey—one that unfolds in every season of life.

The Seasons of Personal Growth

Within the context of "Year Round," the chapter unfolds as a reflection on the seasons of personal growth. Drawing parallels between nature's cycles and the human experience, you are guided through the metaphorical spring of new beginnings, the summer of expansion and abundance, the autumn of reflection and harvest, and the winter of introspection and preparation for the next cycle.

The narrative prompts you to recognize the inevitability of change and view each season as an opportunity for new growth. By understanding the cyclical nature of personal development, you are empowered to navigate life's transitions with resilience and optimism.

Financial Resilience Through Seasons

The "Year-Round" journey extends beyond personal growth to encompass financial resilience. This chapter explores strategies for maintaining financial stability and adapting to economic fluctuations. You are prompted to assess your own financial resilience and implement strategies to safeguard your economic well-being year-round.

Nurturing Relationships Year-Round

As you embark on the year-round journey, the significance of relationships is highlighted. This chapter delves into the interconnectedness of personal and professional connections, emphasizing the role of a supportive network in sustaining transformation. Collaboration, mentorship, and the impact of meaningful relationships underscore that success is often a collective effort.

You are encouraged to cultivate and nurture relationships year-round, recognizing that a strong support system contributes not only to personal well-being but also to the longevity of financial success. The narrative serves as a reminder that the journey from heartache to M.O.N.E.Y. is enriched when shared with others who uplift, inspire, and contribute to your growth.

The Legacy of Purposeful Living

Let's explore how you can leave a lasting impact by aligning your actions and pursuits with a greater purpose. By creating legacies through philanthropy, mentorship, and contributions to your community, you are being inspired to consider the imprint you want to leave on the world.

The "Year-Round" concept becomes a beacon, guiding you to envision a life where the pursuit of prosperity is not only about personal gain but also about making a meaningful difference in the lives of others. I challenge you to define your own legacy, emphasizing that the transformative journey extends beyond your success to the positive influence you can have on the world.

The Journey Continues: Year After Year

As we close this chapter, carry with you the understanding that the journey is not finite but an ongoing exploration of personal and financial growth. The "Year-Round" concept should become a mantra, encouraging you to embrace the ebb and flow of life, adapt to change, and continuously pursue purposeful living.

CHAPTER HIGHLIGHTS

1. **Resilience and Adaptability**

- Throughout the year showcases your resilience and ability to adapt to challenges. Each season becomes a metaphor for evolving strategies and your determination to thrive despite setbacks.

2. **Creative Flourish in Spring**

   - Spring symbolizes a period of creative bloom. Use the season's energy to foster collaboration by bringing together a community of like-minded people to exchange ideas.

3. **Summer Festivals and Business Expansion**

   - Capitalizes on the vibrancy of summer to organize activities to attract clients and collaborators. Let the longer days and warm weather become a catalyst for your expansion, reaching new heights in living your dreams.

4. **Autumn's Transformative Power**

   - As autumn arrives, embrace change and diversify your services to meet the evolving needs of others. This season becomes a metaphor for adaptability and the transformative power of navigating challenges.

5. **Winter Reflection and Mentorship**

   - Winter provides a reflective period for you. Take the time to share your experiences and guide others through the path you have traveled, with a sense of accomplishment and a recognition that success is a continuous journey.

THOUGHT QUESTIONS

1. Reflect on the idea of "Year Round Prosperity." How does the chapter redefine prosperity as a continuous journey rather than a momentary achievement?

   - Consider the stories and examples in the chapter that highlight the concept of sustained growth throughout the seasons. How does this perspective shift the traditional notion of prosperity?

2. Explore the intersection of passion and profit in the pursuit of year-round success. How can you align your passions with profitable ventures for sustained fulfillment?

   - Delve into the narratives that depict you turning your hobbies and interests into year-round opportunities. How can you identify and cultivate opportunities that align with your passions for long-term success?

3. Consider the role of resilience in achieving year-round prosperity. How do setbacks and challenges contribute to long-term growth and success?

   - Reflect on the stories of resilience presented in the chapter. In what ways do challenges become integral parts of the transformative journey toward sustained prosperity?

4. Examine the theme of adaptability in the year-round landscape. How does the chapter emphasize the importance of adaptability in navigating the evolving seasons of life?

   - Explore the examples that underscore the significance of adaptability. How can you develop the capacity to adapt to changing circumstances and seize opportunities throughout the year?

5. Reflect on the holistic approach to life presented in the chapter. How can you integrate the principles of Making, Opportunities, Now, Everywhere, and Year-Round Prosperity into your daily life?

   - Consider the integration of M.O.N.E.Y. Mastery principles discussed in the chapter. How can you apply these principles to create a holistic and fulfilling life journey?

CHAPTER SIX

M.O.N.E.Y.

*I*n *the symphony of M.O.N.E.Y., making opportunities now everywhere year-round, we conduct the transformative melody that echoes beyond financial success, embracing a holistic and fulfilling life journey."*

The office buzzed with anticipation as I sat amidst a sea of paperwork, my fingers dancing across the keyboard. The journey that began with shattered dreams and tear-stained nights had now led me to a place I never imagined – the helm of my own non-profit organization, "Righteous Uplifting Nourishing International, Inc."

In the early days, the prospect of starting a global non-profit seemed daunting, almost impossible. Yet, the burning desire to make a meaningful impact fueled my determination. The philosophy of M.O.N.E.Y. had taken root in my life, and it was time to extend its transformative reach beyond my personal narrative.

The first step involved navigating the labyrinth of legalities and bureaucracy. I found myself immersed in the intricacies of establishing a non-profit – drafting mission statements, building a board of directors, and securing the necessary accreditations. It was a meticulous process, but the vision of Making Opportunities Now Everywhere Year-Round spurred me forward.

"Righteous Uplifting Nourishing International, Inc.," was born, a non-profit dedicated to providing mental health resources to underserved communities worldwide. The initial challenges were met with resilience, mirroring the personal journey that led me to this point. I reached out to individuals who shared the same passion, forming a team that believed in the transformative power of healing.

Our activities were not confined to a specific region or season. The philosophy of "Everywhere" and "Year-Round Prosperity" became the guiding lights for "Righteous Uplifting Nourishing International, Inc."We orchestrated art therapy workshops in disaster-stricken areas, offered counseling services in communities facing socio-economic challenges, and initiated global campaigns to raise awareness about mental health.

The impact began to unfold through the stories of those we touched. Communities once plagued by silence started speaking up, sharing their struggles, and finding solace in the support networks we created. "Righteous Uplifting Nourishing International, Inc." was not just about offering aid; it was about fostering a sense of community and empowerment.

I vividly remember a moment during one of our international workshops. A young artist from a war-torn region painted a mural depicting resilience, hope, and the power of transformation. It was a poignant reminder that the principles of M.O.N.E.Y. were not just theoretical; they were breathing life into communities, turning pain into purpose.

The journey was not without its challenges. Fundraising became an art of its own, requiring creativity and perseverance. Yet, the stories of transformation fueled our determination. We collaborated with local organizations, leveraging global networks to amplify our impact.

As "Righteous Uplifting Nourishing International, Inc." continued to grow, so did the threads connecting hearts across the globe. Each success story, each community touched, reinforced the belief that M.O.N.E.Y. was not just about financial prosperity; it was about enriching lives and fostering a collective sense of well-being.

As I stood before a world map adorned with threads connecting different regions, I marveled at the profound impact that Making Opportunities Now Everywhere Year-Round had on my life and the lives of countless others. The journey from personal heartache to global healing was a testament to the transformative power of M.O.N.E.Y. – a philosophy that transcended individual narratives and stitched a tapestry of resilience, hope, and collective transformation.

Making Opportunities: The Proactive Pursuit of Possibilities

At its core, Making Opportunities is a mindset that rejects passivity and embraces the proactive pursuit of possibilities. It's about acknowledging the inherent power within you to create opportunities, regardless of external circumstances. This involves cultivating a creative outlook, recognizing potential where others see obstacles, and being open to innovative solutions.

A person embodying the Making Opportunities mindset is not a victim of circumstances but a master of adaptation, turning setbacks into stepping stones and challenges into chances for growth. It's an entrepreneurial spirit that constantly seeks avenues for improvement, innovation, and the creation of meaningful opportunities.

Navigating Now and Everywhere: The Dynamic Dance of Adaptability

The concept of Navigating Now and Everywhere emphasizes the importance of being present in the moment while remaining attuned to opportunities that exist everywhere, transcending geographical and situational boundaries. It's a dynamic dance of adaptability, where you navigate the complexities of the present while keeping an eye on the vast landscape of possibilities.

Navigating Now involves making strategic decisions based on current circumstances, and understanding that the ability to adapt to the ever-changing present is a key driver of success. Simultaneously, the idea of Everywhere encourages you to broaden your horizons, explore diverse avenues, and recognize that opportunities are not confined to specific domains but exist ubiquitously.

Year-Round Prosperity: Sustaining Success Across Seasons

Year-Round Prosperity is the culmination of Making Opportunities and Navigating Now and Everywhere. It recognizes that true prosperity is not a momentary achievement but a continuous journey that spans seasons of change. It involves cultivating resilience, planning for long-term success, and adapting strategies to ensure sustained growth.

In the pursuit of Year-Round Prosperity, you learn to view challenges as opportunities for growth, understanding that setbacks are integral parts of the transformative journey. This concept encourages a strategic, forward-thinking approach that goes beyond immediate gains, focusing on the creation of a resilient and thriving future.

Reflection and Integration: Weaving the Threads of Mastery

The final aspect of M.O.N.E.Y. Mastery involves reflection and integration. It prompts you to internalize the principles of Making Opportunities, Navigating Now and Everywhere, and Year-Round Prosperity into your life. It's about weaving the threads of this philosophy into the fabric of your existence, creating a tapestry of resilience, innovation, and continuous growth.

Reflection encourages you to assess your progress, celebrate achievements, and learn from challenges. Integration involves applying the insights gained into daily practices, fostering a mindset that actively seeks and creates opportunities, navigates the present with purpose, and cultivates prosperity year-round.

In essence, M.O.N.E.Y. Mastery is not just about financial success; it's a comprehensive approach to life that empowers you to craft your destiny, adapt to change, and thrive continuously, regardless of the season. It's a philosophy that transcends monetary gain, guiding you toward a fulfilling and prosperous life journey.

CHAPTER HIGHLIGHTS

1. **Proactive Mindset**

   - Explore the proactive mindset of Making Opportunities, emphasizing the rejection of passivity and the active pursuit of possibilities.

   - Illustrate how this mindset empowers individuals to be masters of adaptation, turning challenges into chances for growth and setbacks into stepping stones.

2. **Dynamic Adaptability**

   - Navigate the concept of Navigating Now and Everywhere as a dynamic dance of adaptability.

   - Emphasize the importance of being present in the moment (Now) while remaining open to opportunities everywhere, transcending geographical and situational boundaries.

3. **Year-Round Prosperity**

   - Delve into Year-Round Prosperity as the culmination of Making Opportunities and Navigating Now and Everywhere.

   - Showcase how this concept promotes sustained success across seasons, encouraging resilience, long-term planning, and adaptable strategies.

4. **Reflection and Integration**

   - Highlight the significance of reflection and integration in M.O.N.E.Y. Mastery.

   - Illustrate how you can weave the principles of Making Opportunities, Navigating Now and Everywhere, and Year-Round Prosperity into your life.

5. **Comprehensive Life Approach**

   - Emphasize that M.O.N.E.Y. Mastery goes beyond financial success, offering a comprehensive approach to life.

   - Conclude by presenting M.O.N.E.Y. Mastery as a philosophy that empowers you to craft your destiny, adapt to change, and thrive continuously, irrespective of the season.

THOUGHT QUESTIONS

1. Reflect on the concept of M.O.N.E.Y. Mastery introduced in the chapter. How does this comprehensive approach go beyond financial success to encompass various aspects of life?

   - Consider the holistic philosophy of M.O.N.E.Y. Mastery. In what ways does it empower you to craft your destiny, adapt to change, and thrive continuously?

2. Explore the idea of Making Opportunities as a mindset. How can you cultivate a proactive approach to creating opportunities, especially in the face of adversity?

   - Delve into the principles of Making Opportunities. How can you embody a mindset that actively seeks and generates opportunities, turning challenges into chances for growth?

3. Examine the dynamic dance of adaptability in Navigating Now and Everywhere. How can you navigate the complexities of the present while remaining open to possibilities that exist everywhere?

   - Reflect on the interconnected themes of Navigating Now and Everywhere. How can adaptability be a key driver in successfully navigating the current moment while exploring diverse opportunities?

4. Consider Year-Round Prosperity as a continuous journey. How does the chapter encourage a strategic, forward-thinking approach that extends beyond immediate gains to ensure sustained growth?

    ▪ Explore the concept of Year-Round Prosperity. In what ways can you plan for long-term success, view challenges as opportunities, and adapt strategies for sustained growth throughout the seasons?

5. Reflect on the integration of Making, Opportunities, Now, Everywhere, and Year-Round Prosperity into daily life. How can you weave these principles into your existence for a resilient and thriving future?

    ▪ Delve into the idea of reflection and integration. How can you internalize the principles discussed in the book, applying them to create a tapestry of resilience, innovation, and continuous growth?

CONCLUSION

In the conclusion of "Turning Heartache into M.O.N.E.Y.," we reflect on the transformative journey that has unfolded across the six chapters. The narrative has taken us from the initial steps of creation and innovation in the face of heartache, through the exploration of opportunities, the embrace of the present moment, the recognition of possibilities everywhere, and the commitment to a year-round journey of growth and prosperity.

The overarching message is one of empowerment—a call to action for you to recognize your inherent capacity to turn challenges into opportunities, pain into purpose, and heartache into a catalyst for positive change. The book has served as a guide, offering insights, strategies, and real-life examples to inspire and guide you on your transformative journey.

As we conclude, it is clear that the journey from heartache to M.O.N.E.Y. is not a one-time event but a continuous exploration. The concept of "Year Round" encapsulates the idea that transformation is not bound by specific timelines or limited to particular circumstances—it is a perpetual cycle of growth, adaptation, and purposeful living.

The stories shared throughout the book underscore the resilience of the human spirit, the creativity inherent in adversity, and the endless possibilities awaiting those willing to explore uncharted territories. The lessons of mindfulness, opportunism, adaptability, and the interconnectedness of personal and financial success resonate as enduring principles that extend beyond the pages of the book.

As you close this chapter of your own life, you are invited to carry the spirit of transformation forward. The journey may be challenging at times, but the narrative reinforces the idea that every setback is an opportunity, every moment is a chance for growth, and every season brings new possibilities.

"Turning Heartache into M.O.N.E.Y." is not just a book; it's a roadmap for living a life of purpose, resilience, and prosperity. Leaving you with a sense of empowerment, armed with the knowledge that the journey continues beyond the confines of these pages.

The transformative narrative is ongoing, year after year, offering the promise of a life shaped by intentional choices, continuous learning, and a commitment to turning every experience, no matter how challenging, into a source of strength and opportunity.

Tarrent 'Authur' Henry

MEET THE AUTHOR

Tarrent 'Authur' Henry a/k/a Tarrent-Arthur Henry stands as a distinguished best-selling author, mental wellness specialist, and advocate dedicated to empowering those unfamiliar with mental health resources. Alongside his acclaimed book, "Transforming Heartache into H.O.P.E.," Tarrent-'Authur' introduces his latest work, "Turning Heartache into M.O.N.E.Y. (Making Opportunities Now Everywhere Year-Round)."

In this transformative book, he offers insightful strategies on leveraging challenges for financial success. His diverse expertise encompasses roles as a Best-Selling Author, Poet, Pastor, Chaplain, Mental Wellness Specialist, and advocate and as a Certified Coach, Speaker, Teacher, Trainer, and Facilitator with Maxwell Leadership.

Recognized as a member of Forbes BLK, Tarrent-'Authur' and his wife Helen were named among Success Magazine's 125 most influential entrepreneurs of 2022. Featured in De Mode Magazine in 2023, he continues to contribute significantly to literature and entrepreneurship. Additionally, Tarrent 'Authur' serves as an Executive Contributor to Brainz Magazine, further solidifying his influence in the mental wellness and personal development space.

As the founder of 'Righteous Uplifting Nourishing International, Inc.,' a 501c3 Non-Profit Organization, Tarrent-

'Authur' is committed to empowering individuals globally and making a positive impact on the world.

His earlier book, "The Greatest Truth in the Universe," resonates globally, and "The Wellness Paradigm" establishes him as a leading authority on mental wellness. With "Turning Heartache into M.O.N.E.Y.," Tarrent-'Authur' expands his reach, offering a blueprint for financial success through resilience and resourcefulness.

Embark on your journey to transformation, financial empowerment, and holistic well-being with Tarrent-'Authur' Henry and his groundbreaking books.

Connect with the author or explore more about his work via:

Email Address: info@authurhenry.com

Website: www.authurhenry.com | www.intlrun.org

Brainz Magazine: Author Profile on Brainz Magazine

Unlock Your True Potential - Become the Ideal Human in 90 Days!

Are you ready to transform your life and become the best version of yourself? In just 90 days, my coaching program can empower you to achieve mental, emotional, physical, and spiritual well-being while cultivating a strong relationship with God. Say goodbye to feeling unwell and unfulfilled—start your journey toward becoming the ideal human today!

What You'll Gain:

- **Mental Wellness:** Develop tools to enhance your mental clarity and resilience.

- **Emotional Well-being:** Learn strategies to manage emotions and build emotional intelligence.

- **Physical Health:** Achieve optimal physical well-being through personalized guidance.

- **Spiritual Wholeness:** Strengthen your connection with God and nurture your spiritual growth.

- Why Choose My Program:

- **Holistic Approach:** Addressing every aspect of your well-being for comprehensive transformation.

- **Practical Tools:** Learn practical, actionable strategies for immediate impact.

- **Tailored Guidance:** Personalized coaching to meet your unique needs and goals.

- **Efficient Transformation:** Witness significant changes in just 90 days.

Don't let another day pass without taking control of your life. Embrace the opportunity to be the ideal human you've always aspired to be. Visit my website www.authurhenry.com to get started on your transformative journey today.

Unlock your true potential and become the ideal human you were meant to be!